My mum went to hospital
to have a baby.

My mum had a baby boy.
She came home
with my dad.

The baby is very little.
He has a dress on.

4 My mum is happy
my dad is happy
and I am happy.

The baby is not happy. 5
He is crying.
He wants some milk.

My mum has a bottle
for the baby.

She puts warm milk
in the bottle
and gives it to the baby.

The baby drinks his milk.

I can hold
the baby.

10 He is a good baby.
He goes to sleep.

Our baby sleeps
in a little cot.

I have to look after
the baby.

We show our baby
to all the people
in our street.

When he gets big
I will play with him.

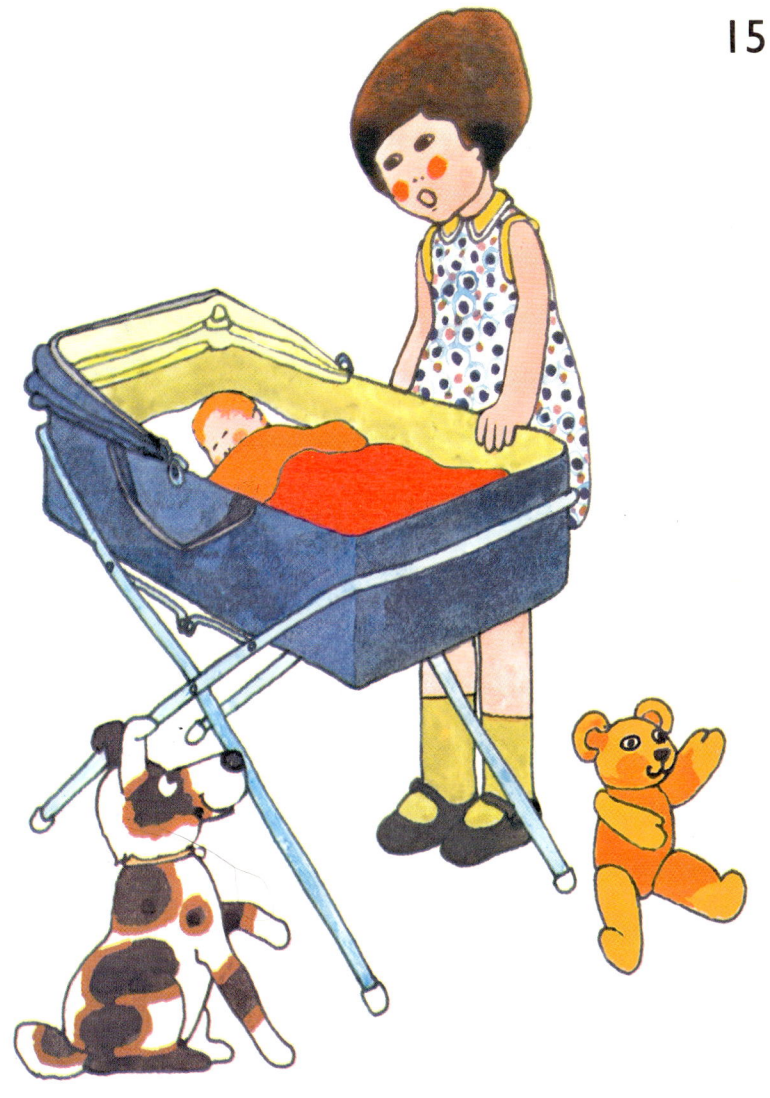

I sing our baby to sleep.

Rock a bye baby
On the tree top.
When the wind blows
The cradle will rock.
When the bough breaks
The cradle will fall.
Down will come baby
Cradle and all.